EFFECTIVE
PUBLIC RELATIONS

MOI ALI

D1009038

Senior Art Editor Jamie Hanson
Senior Editor Nina Hathway
DTP Designer Amanda Peers
Production Controller Michelle Thomas

Managing Editor Adèle Hayward
Senior Managing Editor Stephanie Jackson
Senior Managing Art Editor Nigel Duffield
US Editors Gary Werner, Margaret Parrish

Produced for Dorling Kindersley by

COOLING BROWN
9–11 High Street, Hampton
Middlesex TW12 2SA

Creative Director Arthur Brown
Senior Editor Amanda Lebentz

First American Edition, 2001

01 02 03 04 05 10 9 8 7 6 5 4 3 2 1

Published in the United States by
DK Publishing, Inc.
95 Madison Avenue,
New York, New York 10016

A Cataloging in Publication record is available from
the Library of Congress

ISBN 0-7894-8008-5

Reproduced by Colourscan, Singapore
Printed and bound in Hong Kong by Wing King Tong

See our complete catalog at
www.dk.com

CONTENTS

DEVELOPING PR SKILLS

WORKING WITH THE MEDIA

INTRODUCTION

Public relations comprises a set of practical skills and strategies designed to enhance the reputation of an organization, strengthen its relationships with key audiences, and enable it to deal with crises from a position of strength. Whether PR is the main focus of your work, or merely an addition to your job description, Effective Public Relations will guide you to success. Covering the principal aspects of PR, including the vital skills of using the media, organizing events, and producing persuasive publicity material, this book shows you how to ensure the wellbeing of your organization. Use the self-assessment questionnaire to measure your skill level and identify areas for improvement; and follow the hints, guidance, and advice to help you build and develop your PR skills. Backed up with 101 tips, this book is an invaluable pocket guide to an essential business discipline.

UNDERSTANDING PUBLIC RELATIONS

An organization's reputation is one of its most critical assets. Understand how public relations builds and enhances a good image and why a strategic approach ensures success.

DEFINING PUBLIC RELATIONS

Public relations, or PR, is a powerful tool that can make a vital contribution to organizational success. Learn to distinguish between effective PR and cheap publicity gimmicks in order to build a solid, respected reputation with your key audiences.

1 Be aware that an organization's actions can have wide implications.

UNDERSTANDING THE BASICS

Public relations describes the way issues and messages are communicated between an organization and the public. It is the discipline that looks after corporate reputation. The aim of PR is to win understanding and support from, and to influence the opinions and behavior of, an organization's key audiences. This is achieved through a planned, sustained set of activities.

2 Make certain that all PR claims can be substantiated.

BUILDING REPUTATION

The true purpose of PR is to create a well-deserved reputation. That may involve offering excellent customer care, communicating effectively with your audiences, and showing social responsibility toward your workforce, the local community, and the environment. Cheap publicity gimmicks designed to deceive the public, or glitzy activities aimed at diverting attention from poor organizational behavior, give PR a bad name and have no place in an effective PR campaign.

3 Remind colleagues that they all have a PR role, regardless of their job title.

ANTICIPATING EVENTS

Effective PR is about anticipating tomorrow's issues, rather than apologizing to staff and the public for poor decisions that have been made. By harnessing PR skills you will not only be able to act to improve the reputation of your organization, but you will also be able to show your colleagues what PR can do to make their jobs easier. Demonstrate how PR can help the human resources department improve employee communications. Prove the worth of PR in supporting marketing activity. Ensure that the chief executive knows that good PR can build better investor relationships and thereby help the stock price.

4 Know that averting bad publicity is as crucial as attracting good publicity.

▼ **ACHIEVING A GOOD OUTCOME**
The outcome of effective PR is a good, well-deserved image based on a genuine commitment to provide excellent service and to be a good, caring employer and a responsible organization. Cheap publicity creates an image without substance.

POSITIVE OUTCOME

"I like that organization"

"The staff are genuine and I trust them"

"It deserves its good reputation"

POOR OUTCOME

"That company always hypes its achievements"

"This is just another cheap PR stunt"

"It uses glossy publicity to hide its shortcomings"

USING PR WITH MARKETING

The differences between PR and marketing may seem blurred, yet each has its own part to play in organizational success. Use PR to support marketing activity and coordinate these two distinct disciplines for maximum impact.

> **5** Use both editorial and advertising to secure positive media coverage.

FITTING PR INTO THE MARKETING MIX

Marketing involves developing the right product at the right price, getting it to a place where consumers can buy it, and promoting it so that they know about it. These components are known as the marketing mix, or the four Ps: product, price, place, and promotion. PR is often seen as the fifth P of the mix, standing for perception. Consumers prefer to do business with organizations they hold in high regard, and effective PR builds positive perceptions, creating a fertile environment for successful marketing.

WORKING WITH THE MARKETING TEAM ▼
Attend marketing meetings, explain to marketing colleagues how PR can support their campaigns, and point out any negative PR implications that may result from their planned activity.

Marketing manager looks for ways of attracting media attention

> **6** Plan a day away with colleagues to improve team dynamics.

SUPPORTING MARKETING OBJECTIVES WITH PR

MARKETING OBJECTIVE	SUPPORTIVE PR ACTIVITY
To build stronger and more lasting relationships with clients.	● Organize a corporate hospitality event. ● Produce a quarterly customer newsletter.
To increase the public's awareness of the organization.	● Secure positive media coverage. ● Organize an open day.
To promote a new line of products more widely.	● Secure editorial in trade and consumer press. ● Organize in-store tastings or trial sessions.

7 Ask for a copy of your organization's marketing strategy.

WORKING TOGETHER

For maximum impact, PR and marketing activity should be coordinated. When the marketing department advertises new products and services, reinforce the campaign by attracting favorable editorial coverage. Use your company website as a marketing tool as well as a PR vehicle. Create an area for journalists with press releases, background information, and press photographs for downloading. Combined PR and marketing campaigns can be worth far more than the sum of their individual parts.

Marketing team member explains new campaign

PR executive explains how a press release will help

COMMUNICATING EFFECTIVELY

Public relations is really about communication because effective dialogue lies at its heart. To ensure success, make sure that communication is a two-way process, and be aware of nonverbal and unintentional messages.

 8 Examine the way in which your customers perceive you.

9 To communicate well, be prompt, accurate, and comprehensive.

UNDERSTANDING COMMUNICATION

Good communication enables you to build lasting relationships with your target audiences, transform difficult relationships, and avert misunderstanding that leads to ill will. Poor communication leaves customers feeling ignored and reluctant to do business with you again. Assess the effectiveness of all your communication methods, such as letters, emails, face-to-face talks, and publicity materials.

ENSURING TWO-WAY COMMUNICATION

Remember that communication is a two-way process. As well as sending out the right messages, an organization must establish mechanisms to receive them from others, including staff, customers, suppliers, and the public. Make it easy for people to communicate with you. Send out questionnaires to seek feedback. Use comment cards and suggestion boxes. Include an email reply device on your website. When you receive messages, show that you value dialogue by replying promptly to those who took the trouble to contact you.

10 Know when to listen – effective communication is about more than just talking.

SENDING THE RIGHT MESSAGES

Ensure that any messages you convey are by design rather than accident. Burly security men guarding doors; signs curtly stating rules and regulations; or unfriendly, unhelpful, or untrained staff are powerful but negative messages. They send out signals of an unwelcoming or uncaring organization. Do not overlook the impact that actions of staff, or policies and procedures, can have in conveying an unfavorable image. Look at your organization as if for the first time. What is your impression? Gather first impressions from new staff, new customers, or first-time visitors to your premises. Listen to what they say and act to eradicate unintentional negative messages.

QUESTIONS TO ASK YOURSELF

Q Do we always inform customers of delays?

Q Do we always tell customers about changes to arrangements?

Q Do we tell customers about relevant internal news, such as new staff appointments?

11 Ensure that the message sent is the message received.

A lack of eye contact implies a lack of interest

NEGATIVE

UNDERSTANDING ▶ NONVERBAL MESSAGES

Nonverbal messages are very powerful. In these two scenarios, a customer receives very different signals. An uncaring, unfriendly message from a staff member damages her faith in the company, while helpful and considerate body language instills goodwill.

A smile shows pleasure in dealing with the customer

A neat appearance communicates a professional image

POSITIVE

TAKING A
STRATEGIC APPROACH

Long-term, strategic PR planning is far more effective than uncoordinated flurries of activity. Map out your public relations campaign so that your purpose is clear, activity can be planned, progress monitored, and outcomes measured.

12 Ensure that PR strategy supports both corporate and marketing strategies.

13 Use PR proactively to anticipate and avert bad publicity.

14 Take the offensive rather than be on the defensive.

UNDERSTANDING STRATEGY

To achieve a proactive approach to PR, you will need to produce a PR strategy. Your strategy must support your organization's corporate strategy, as well as linking with your company's marketing strategy. Because of this, it can be helpful to involve those responsible for corporate and marketing strategy when planning PR strategy. They can help explain the organization's wider strategy, while you can explain to them how PR can be used to support corporate goals.

SETTING OBJECTIVES

The first step in strategic planning is to establish objectives, a set of goals that define what you want to achieve. These might focus on improving your organization's reputation, raising its profile, or building stronger relationships with key groups, for example. Clear objectives will help you to reach your target, to chart progress, to measure results, and to assess effectiveness. Set objectives at the outset, but make sure that you allow ample time for this. All PR activity that you undertake will be aimed at achieving these goals.

POINTS TO REMEMBER

● Objectives should be clear, specific, unambiguous, quantifiable, and incorporate a time frame.

● To ensure that they remain relevant, objectives should be revised periodically.

● If objectives are to be effective, they should be demanding yet achievable.

15 Use PR persuasively to help shape the way others see your organization.

IDENTIFYING TARGET AUDIENCES

Most organizations will have several audiences or "publics," so a strategic approach to PR involves clearly identifying all of them. Some will be regarded as more important than others. Audiences might include:

● customers;
● staff;
● media;
● public;
● investors/shareholders;
● market analysts;
● other stakeholders;
● the local community;
● local, regional/state, or national/federal government.

16 Define messages to promote what you value and find ways to convey them.

DEFINING KEY MESSAGES

Every organization will have key corporate messages that need to be conveyed. You might, for example, want to tell everyone how innovative your organization is, or how caring. In addition to these, there will be a subset of messages personalized for each principal audience. When launching a new product, for example, investors will want to be told of any impact on the stock price. The media and the community's focus of interest may be on the environmental impact. Try to give each audience information tailored to its particular needs and viewpoint.

▼ **REAPING THE BENEFITS**
In developing a strategic approach and setting aside time for PR, Eileen made a major contribution to the success of the business. Sales continued to increase, and PR came to be regarded as a vital and valued part of the organization's work.

CASE STUDY
Eileen worked for a medium-sized engineering firm. Part of her job was to take care of the company's PR. However, she was so busy with her principal tasks that PR was very much an afterthought. Most of what took place was reactive and defensive, and outcomes were never measured. Thanks to this chaotic, ad hoc approach, PR bore little fruit, confirming a general feeling that PR was a waste of time. Eileen decided to undertake some PR planning. She drew up a strategy and set aside time to implement it. Within a few months, media exposure in the trade press had increased dramatically, leading directly to an upturn in orders. As a result of improved internal communication, production staff felt renewed motivation and accepted new working arrangements in order to meet their bulging workload. Faith in PR grew and Eileen was given a full-time PR role.

17 Consider inviting key colleagues to strategic planning meetings.

PLANNING FOR SUCCESS ▼

Ask the team to suggest effective ways of communicating messages to your principal audiences. Choose a channel that is appropriate to your audience, the message, and the urgency of conveying it.

ACHIEVING OBJECTIVES

Strategic PR involves considerable research, planning, and discussion. How will you meet your objectives? What ideas do you have for conveying the desired messages to your principal audiences. Draw up a series of ideas to help you meet each of your objectives. Calculate the cost of each idea, decide which ones you will implement, then produce an activity timetable. Include details of who will be responsible for each activity, with start and completion dates. Hold regular meetings with those involved in implementation so that you can chart progress and solve any problems.

PR manager favors combining methods for maximum impact

Team member suggests holding an exhibition to promote message

DOCUMENTING THE PLAN

A PR strategy is a written document, not a set of ideas to be carried around in your head. Writing down your strategy also helps you to focus on what you need to achieve, how, and when. Record details of your key publics, along with the principal messages per audience. You will also need to include your objectives, and – in broad terms – your ideas for achieving them. Specify what measures you will use to evaluate success and set a date for an interim evaluation. The final part of the strategy is your activity timetable.

18 Review your PR strategy every six months.

19 Ensure PR activity is geared toward achievement.

ASSESSING EFFECTIVENESS

Measuring effectiveness is an important element of strategic PR. The aim of measuring is to assess whether or not objectives have been achieved. Use questionnaires, focus groups, and other research methods to measure whether your messages have reached their target and achieved the desired outcome. You may need to conduct research before a PR campaign, as well as afterward, to obtain an accurate measure of shifts in behavior or attitude. Use evaluation to learn which tactics and techniques worked, and which did not. This knowledge will help you to be more effective next time.

20 Good PR can reduce staff absenteeism.

21 Look for creative solutions to PR problems.

MEASURING THE EFFECTIVENESS OF A PR CAMPAIGN

INDICATOR	HOW TO MEASURE EFFECTIVENESS
REACH	● How well did the message reach the target audiences? ● What is the proof?
KNOWLEDGE	● How well informed and educated is the audience about the company and its products? ● How do we know?
UNDERSTANDING	● Has the audience grasped the message? ● How can we tell?
PREFERENCE	● Has favor increased with the target audience? ● How do we know?
ATTITUDES	● Has the audience's view been altered in a positive way? ● Is there any evidence of this?
OPINIONS	● Have people's opinions changed in the way that was intended? ● How do we know?
BEHAVIOR	● Has target audience behavior altered in the intended way? ● How do we know?

DEVELOPING PR SKILLS

Improving staff communication and customer care, dealing with crises, and organizing events and campaigns are key PR skills. Learn how to become an accomplished PR practitioner.

COMMUNICATING WITH STAFF

Good PR starts at home. Committed and helpful staff create a good image, so regard employees not just as a workforce, but as a principal target audience. Nurture staff commitment through effective employee communication involving genuine dialogue.

22 Ask staff for their ideas on how communication can be improved.

23 Communicate well to reduce staff turnover and boost morale.

KEEPING STAFF INFORMED

Use PR techniques to help you achieve a genuine and meaningful relationship with staff. Employees need to know what is going on in their organization and should be kept informed at an early stage of developments that will affect them. Tell employees about new staff, promotions, job opportunities, new products and services, high-profile marketing activity, financial results, and future plans. Effective internal communication is in everyone's interests.

CREATING REAL DIALOGUE

Recognize the benefits of sharing information and create a genuine, open, two-way communication channel between staff and management. Staff are sometimes skeptical of internal communication because it is often used merely to deliver bad news, such as layoffs. Distrust is understandable if staff receive nothing but company propaganda. Staff want to hear all news, good and bad, presented in a straightforward and honest way. Ensure that the information flow is two-way. All team members can provide valuable insights. Encourage them to feed ideas to managers.

> **24** Present information in a way that is easy to understand.

> **25** Avoid using euphemisms in an attempt to dilute bad news.

QUESTIONS TO ASK YOURSELF

Q What are the different categories of employee?

Q What does each group need to know?

Q What is the preferred manner of communication?

Q How can we improve the ways in which we communicate?

UNDERTAKING A COMMUNICATIONS AUDIT

You may be surprised at how staff regard the effectiveness or otherwise of your organization's internal communication. Find out what your staff think. Where are the information blockages? Are you telling staff too much or too little? Do they understand and believe the corporate messages? Demonstrate to staff that their views are important. Send out a questionnaire, phrasing questions so that you can identify where the problems are. Act on the findings. Draw up an action plan, share it with staff, then implement it.

◀ **BEING OPEN**
Spike's reluctance to discuss bad news with staff led to fear, insecurity, and the loss of a team member. By talking to his employees, Spike put an end to all the worrying and ensured their continued support.

CASE STUDY
Spike owned and managed a small record production company employing 25 staff. A former artist was taking him to court over a disagreement about royalties. Upset about the court case, Spike kept this news to himself. But gossip in the industry eventually reached Spike's employees. They began to worry about the future of their jobs: rumor suggested that the legal action could bankrupt Spike. One staff member who was offered a job elsewhere decided to accept because of the feared uncertainty of her current job. Overhearing the office gossip, Spike realized that a wholly inaccurate story was circulating. He called a meeting to explain the situation. Staff learned that Spike was the wronged party and stood an excellent chance of winning his court battle. Morale improved and staff were able to support Spike through this difficult time.

MANAGING YOUR CORPORATE REPUTATION

A good corporate image is founded on substance, and its creation should be more than a cosmetic exercise. Assess your current image carefully, draw up an action plan to tackle weak areas, and then work hard to maintain your reputation.

26 Tackle complaints from customers promptly and considerately.

27 Always aim to exceed customer expectations.

▼ **CREATING AN IMAGE MATRIX**
This sample shows a simple matrix that you can adapt to suit your needs and use to help you plan action after undertaking an image audit within your organization.

CONDUCTING AN IMAGE AUDIT

Find out how your audiences perceive you, using research methods such as questionnaires and focus groups. Combine this with an audit of your main methods of communication. Look for unintentional messages. What message is conveyed by a dirty delivery van, for example? Examine every aspect of your work that communicates something about your organization, including premises, policies, and customer care. Ask yourself, "With only this to go on, what would I think of us as an organization?"

	ITEM 1	ITEM 2	ITEM 3
Item examined	Lobby area	Promotional brochure	Delivery waiting times for customers
Image conveyed	Dowdy and old-fashioned	Cheap and unprofessional	Inefficient and unprofessional
Desired image	Welcoming and stylish	Attractive, professional, and upmarket	Fast, efficient, and customer-oriented
Action required	Redecorate and replace chairs	Produce new brochure with good design	Explore recruiting more free-lance and part-time packers
Budget	$1,200	$18,000	Unknown
Delegated to	Melanie	Stephen	Mark
Start/completion	Feb/March	March/June	Feb/March

ENGENDERING TRUST

Organizations with good reputations are trusted. It pays to engender trust because:

- People are more likely to do business with you;
- They are more likely to buy your stocks;
- You attract better staff;
- The media and the public trust you to tell the truth;
- You are more likely to be believed in times of adversity.

PRODUCING AN ACTION PLAN

Having identified the shortcomings in your image, you now need to tackle these weaknesses by devising practical ideas and incorporating them into a workable action plan aimed at improving perceptions. Ensure that every action in your plan is assigned to a named person with the skills, the authority, and the time to carry it out. Give those responsible for implementation a sufficient budget, and agree a to start and a completion date. Bring them together for a briefing; they need to be able to see the big picture and understand the reasoning behind the need for action. Ask for progress updates so that you can monitor implementation.

MAINTAINING A REPUTATION

It can take years to build a good image, but a reputation can be destroyed in seconds. Work to maintain your hard-won image. Show staff that you value them, treat them well, and communicate openly with them. Unhappy staff tell their friends how dissatisfied they are, thus damaging your reputation as a good employer. Disaffected staff also tend to provide poor service, which will erode your good image. Provide excellent customer care so that people have no cause to complain; when complaints do occur, make sure that you handle them swiftly, fairly, and courteously.

▼ CREATING AN OVERLAP

To maintain a successful reputation, there must be an overlap between the identity that an organization seeks to create and the image it has with the public, so that their experience of the organization tallies with the way in which it is publicized.

Radio safety campaign promotes the image of a caring organization

CARING FOR CUSTOMERS

Excellent customer care is at the very core of effective PR. Your reputation depends upon it. Aim to attain 100 percent customer satisfaction by training staff, introducing a customer charter, and taking prompt action to rectify mistakes.

28 Try to ensure that your customers have nothing to complain about.

29 Turn dissatisfied customers into advocates.

30 Try to see matters from a customer's perspective.

DELIVERING EXCELLENT SERVICE

One of the best ways to build or enhance a good image is to work hard at getting your customer care right. Conversely, ignore customer care and you will damage your reputation. It is surprising how few staff seem able to provide good service naturally. Most need training. Additionally, they must feel committed and motivated. Check that staff know what is expected of them. Produce a set of measurable service standards and offer incentives to meet them.

DEVELOPING A CUSTOMER CHARTER

Draw up a customer charter that tells customers what they can expect from you and what you will do if you fail to keep your promise. Provided that you deliver on your customer charter commitments, this can be an excellent way of enhancing your reputation and giving people confidence in you. Specify how quickly you will answer the phone; reply to letters, faxes, and emails; and deliver orders. Produce a clear, fair complaints procedure and a return policy for faulty or unwanted goods. Make sure that you give people confidence to do business with you again and again.

QUESTIONS TO ASK YOURSELF

Q Do our customers have strong reasons to recommend us to others?

Q Have we reassured customers with guarantees of what we will do if things go wrong?

31 Make customer satisfaction the goal of all staff.

BEING ACCOMMODATING

Adopt a "can do" attitude. Sometimes an organization's rules and regulations, policies, and procedures get in the way of good customer service. Insisting that all inquiries are submitted in writing is an example of an inflexible and unfriendly rule. Check your own rules for customer friendliness: are they entirely necessary? Be prepared to be flexible where you can. Train staff to be genuinely helpful and to accommodate all reasonable customer requests. Go that extra mile to make a customer happy. Total customer satisfaction should be the goal of all staff.

Team member learns how to ask a customer if they need help

32 Avoid passing customers from one department to another.

Trainer intervenes in role play to suggest a more helpful approach

◀ INVESTING IN CUSTOMER CARE
Expert customer care training is an investment, not a cost. Remember that all new staff should undergo training in the organization's customer care program, and existing staff may need refresher training every two or three years.

Colleague gives feedback in her role as customer

PLANNING A CAMPAIGN

Campaigning is becoming increasingly popular as a method of raising an organization's profile and building a positive image. Plan your campaign carefully, launch it in a blaze of publicity, and know how to sustain it until your objectives are achieved.

33 To be sure of success, plan your campaign with military precision.

34 Work out your budget carefully – campaigning can be expensive.

ADDRESSING THE FUNDAMENTALS

Organizations may campaign in support of a consumer issue, or they may join forces with other organizations to mount a trade campaign to promote their industry or to lobby local, national, or international government on an issue that affects their industry. Before contemplating a campaign launch, consider all the issues. Decide on your objectives (what you want to achieve); target (whom you want to influence); and tactics and techniques (how you will achieve your objectives). You should also examine the strengths and weaknesses of your case, gather your facts, and anticipate opposing arguments.

RECOGNIZING A GOOD CAMPAIGNER ▼
The hallmarks of a good campaigner are easy to spot. They are creative, committed, and highly effective individuals with logical minds and often with infectious enthusiasm. These qualities will stand them in good stead when charged with running a campaign.

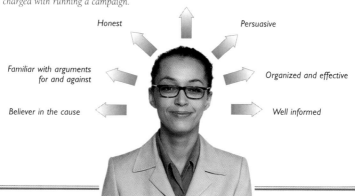

Articulate

Honest

Persuasive

Familiar with arguments for and against

Organized and effective

Believer in the cause

Well informed

NAMING YOUR CAMPAIGN

It is always advisable to name your campaign. This can help turn a rather nebulous set of objectives into an entity with its own distinct identity, making it easier for supporters to identify with your cause. Campaign names should be apt, memorable, and preferably short. Add further character to your campaign by designing a logo and visual identity that can be used on stationery and other materials to help promote and reinforce the campaign aims. A slogan that encapsulates the campaign aims in a snappy way is also a good idea.

35 Publicize campaign successes to rekindle interest.

36 Organize a campaign launch and invite the media along.

PRODUCING MATERIALS

Most campaigns require some type of literature aimed at informing and educating, persuading and winning support, and publicizing aims. This might include a campaign leaflet setting out your case; posters and other promotional material; and balloons, buttons, pens, and carrier bags stamped with the campaign slogan. A campaign video is a good way of spreading the word. If you wish to encourage supporters to join in the campaigning activity, produce a campaign pack outlining how they can demonstrate their support, and provide factsheets containing the information they will need when speaking out in your favor.

SUSTAINING INTEREST

By mapping out campaign activity well into the future, you will ensure that your campaign does not peter out after a successful launch. Make a timetable of the activities you will undertake in the weeks and months after the launch. Create opportunities to attract publicity and spread the campaign message. Do research and publicize the findings. Think of ideas for photo ops. Mount displays and exhibitions. Start a petition.

37 Use creativity and inventiveness to keep your cause in the limelight.

ORGANIZING EVENTS

Much PR activity is event based, making event management a fundamental PR skill. Come up with a creative idea for an event, select your venue with care, and plan down to the very last detail to ensure a day to remember.

38 Involve helpers at an early stage in the planning of a new event.

39 Try to be original when planning an event in order to make it memorable.

40 Choose a venue or celebrity guest to link with the theme of your event.

PLANNING AN EVENT

There are all manner of PR events that you may consider planning, from product launches and factory, store, or new office openings to parties, open days, corporate entertainment, exhibitions, open days, press conferences, and media trips. Events are organized to profile-raise, build customer loyalty, and enhance reputation. Some events require no more than organizational skills; others call for creativity, too. On occasion, you will need to come up with interesting, original, and appropriate ideas for memorable events. This might involve reserving an unusual venue – such as a wax museum, movie studios, or butterfly farm – or using a celebrity sportsperson, movie star, or pop singer.

SETTING THE DATE

The date of an event may be predetermined, such as your organization's anniversary. Often, though, you will be able to influence it. If you are able to dictate when an event will occur, aim to make it coincide with another linked or topical occasion. An event for couples may benefit from being held on Valentine's Day, for example. Beware of competing events; it would be unfortunate if someone else's high-profile occasion stole the limelight from your own.

41 Avoid setting an adverse date, such as an outdoor event in winter.

THINGS TO DO

1. Set a date that will not clash with other big events.
2. Choose an appropriate venue for your launch.
3. Decide who to invite – this may include supporters, politicians, and the media.
4. Decide on the form of your launch – press conference, photo op, seminar, or other.

SELECTING A PLANNING COMMITTEE

Small events can easily be managed by one person, but you will need the help and support of others when planning major events. Establish a planning team for significant events, involving people with the time and skills to assist. Look for helpers who are well organized and enthusiastic, and involve them at the earliest stage so that they have a stronger stake in your event's success. It is easy when event planning to overlook small but vital issues, so list what needs to be done, down to the last detail, and ensure that a team member is given responsibility for each item.

BRIEFING KEY PARTICIPANTS

If you are asking people to perform a function at an event – such as giving an after-dinner speech or officiating at an opening – provide a comprehensive brief. This is especially important if they are unfamiliar with your company. The better informed they are, the better they will do the job. Explain, preferably face-to-face, and followed up in writing, what you expect from them. State clearly the purpose of the event, what you want them to do, and who will be there. Specify when they are to arrive, and when they can expect to leave. If necessary, include some background information on your organization, a map, and parking details.

▼ PREPARING MATERIAL FOR A GUEST SPEAKER

Provide your guest speaker with a full script well in advance of the event, setting out the main points to cover. He or she will then be able to prepare notes to make sure that the speech is delivered smoothly.

42 Check speakers' credentials to ensure they have the right expertise.

Speaker uses notes based on organizer's draft to ensure relevance

Booking a Venue

Draw up a list of possible venues so that you can compare the advantages and disadvantages of each, bearing in mind costs, location, capacity, and facilities. Think about the type of atmosphere you wish to create: will it be a serious occasion, or a fun, informal one? The venue will set the mood of your presentation. Consider whether the venue is accessible to your guests – is it within easy reach of public transportation, or will you need to organize transportation?

43 Select a venue that complements your corporate image.

▼ CONFIRMING DETAILS
Whenever you reserve anything – equipment, speakers, venues, food, and so on – always confirm your reservation and all requirements in writing. Keep a record of all correspondence and phone calls.

Dear Janet Smith,

I am writing to confirm the details we discussed when I visited you earlier this week.

I would like to reserve the function suite and the two connecting syndicate rooms at the Grand Hotel for our annual seminar on August 20. We will need the rooms from 9 a.m. to 5 p.m. We will also have sole use of the banqueting suite from 12.30 p.m. to 1.30 p.m. and from 3 p.m. to 3.30 p.m.

Specify all dates and times

There will be 150 people in total, 140 guests plus 10 staff. We require tea, coffee, and cookies for 150 people to be available on arrival of delegates (9.30 a.m., although I will arrive at 9 a.m.). Your staff will serve this in the main function room. As agreed, herbal teas will also be available. Tea, coffee, and cookies will be served again at 3 p.m. in the banqueting suite.

Confirm any special requests

Delegates will move to the banqueting suite at 12.30 p.m. for lunch. We would like menu B. One week before the event I will contact you to confirm the nature and number of special meals. In addition, you will have five surplus vegetarian meals available on the day for delegates who have not confirmed one in advance. One bottle of red house wine will be served to each table of four people. Two bottles of mineral water will also be available per table. Each table will have a centerpiece of pink carnations.

We will need an overhead projector and screen in each of the three rooms, as well as a flipchart stand, pad, and pens in the two syndicate rooms. We will supply name tags, pads, and pens.

State any equipment you want the venue to provide, and check that any equipment you want to bring is acceptable

Please write to me within the next seven days to confirm that you agree to these arrangements.

I look forward to hearing from you.

Always ask suppliers to write confirming that they agree to providing your specified arrangements

Yours sincerely

Paula Wilson

Paula Wilson
PR Manager

PLANNING THE KEY COMPONENTS OF AN EVENT

KEY COMPONENT	HOW TO PLAN EFFECTIVELY
VENUE The location of an event. This must be chosen carefully to suit the type of function.	Check that a proposed venue can accommodate your needs, that it is large enough for your requirements, and that it can meet any special needs of your guests, such as providing disabled access or aids for the hearing impaired.
CATERING Food and refreshments provided during the event. Quantity, quality, and price are main considerations.	Shop around, as prices vary considerably. Look at sample menus and ensure that people with special dietary needs — vegetarians, vegans, people with food allergies, etc. – can be catered for. Check that the venue allows outside caterers.
GUEST LIST A list of all invitees, including staff such as photographers, and a reserve guest list.	Keep a reserve list so that if a guest is unable to attend, you can diplomatically fill the place with someone from your backup list. Design and print invitations for everyone on the guest list and distribute them in plenty of time.
ENTERTAINMENT Musicians, singers, dancers, comedians, or other performers or activities planned for the event.	Try to see any entertainers in action before you hire them. Find out what facilities entertainers will need, such as a dressing room, a public address system, lighting, backing music, or a nearby power supply.

BEING PREPARED

Draw up a checklist of facilities and equipment needed for your event. This might include: a public address system; portable toilets; tables and chairs; slide or overhead projectors; television and video recorder; lighting; a lectern; badges; tents and marquees; or barriers and signage. You may need staff such as security, technicians, and parking attendants. Pay attention to detail and ensure that nothing is overlooked.

DEALING WITH LEGAL AND SAFETY MATTERS

When you organize an event, you are responsible for the safety of people attending it and must take all reasonable steps to protect them. Investigate what is required to ensure that your event is safe and legal. Local and national laws may apply, perhaps requiring you to obtain a license for public entertainment or the serving of alcohol. Police permission may be needed for certain types of event. There are possible food hygiene laws to consider. You may need security and first aiders. Safety barriers may be necessary. Take care to remain within the law, gain sufficient public liability insurance, and seek the necessary permits. If you are planning a large public event, consider seeking advice from a professional event manager.

Exhibiting at Events

An exhibition provides the opportunity to present your message to the public and inform them of your work. Decide what you want to achieve, select your showcase with care, and undertake careful planning to ensure that you make the most of the event.

44 Carefully consider what you hope to achieve by exhibiting.

Questions to Ask Yourself

Q Why do we want to stage an exhibition or mount a display?

Q What are our main objectives?

Q Is this the best way of achieving them?

Q Will our chosen showcase enable us to reach our target audience?

Should You Exhibit?

Exhibitions aimed at attracting sales – at trade fairs, for example – are usually organized by the marketing department. Exhibitions aimed at persuading, educating, promoting an image, or raising your profile are the domain of PR staff. Buying a stand at an exhibition, staffing it, and producing attractive display boards can be expensive but provides an excellent opportunity to reach your target audience face-to-face and to engage them in discussions about your work.

Choosing a Showcase

The key to successful exhibiting is to select the right venue: one that will attract your target audience. If you plan to display at a major exhibition, ask the organizers for detailed audience profiles to help you decide whether this is a suitable showcase for you. Ask who else will be exhibiting there. Find out about the organizer's promotional strategy (advertising, editorial, leaflets, and so on) for publicizing the event. Be sure that it will attract a big enough turnout of the right kind of people.

LOCATING YOUR STAND ▶
Visit a venue in advance to check the location of your stand. Make sure that your stand occupies a bright, central position, where it will attract the maximum number of visitors.

Staff member presents visitor with a promotional bag containing an information pack and gift

STAFFING YOUR STAND

While informative display boards in your chosen location will promote your message well enough, staffed stands are a more effective (albeit more costly) way of communicating. Select staff who are outgoing, happy to talk to people, and at the right level for the occasion. For example, a stand at a conference for chief executive officers should be staffed by high-ranking individuals who can talk comfortably and knowledgeably with CEOs. Brief staff thoroughly so that they know what message they are promoting, and can answer any likely questions. Organize a staffing schedule to cover rest breaks so that your stand is staffed at all times.

◀ DELIVERING YOUR MESSAGE
Instruct staff on what to do with visitors once they are over the threshold, whether it is to talk through the display or show a video. Visitors should leave the stand carrying your message in their hand or in their head.

ATTRACTING PEOPLE TO YOUR STAND

Staffing a stand can sometimes be a dispiriting matter. People may wander past, but it can be difficult to get them to come over and take a look. Consider how you will attract visitors to your stand. Perhaps you could organize a prize draw, provide free refreshments, or offer a free consultation. What can you place on your stand to act as a people magnet? Interactive computers, demonstrations, talks, and participative workshops can all be used to entice visitors in. Design your stand carefully to ensure that it is accessible, with no barriers to entry, and that it looks attractive, colorful, and appealing. Friendly and approachable staff can also make a big difference to attendance at your stand.

POINTS TO REMEMBER

- Negotiating before paying for a stand will help you to ensure a better deal.
- Your stand and contents should always be insured.
- There should be sufficient supplies of company literature.
- All leads should be followed up after the event.

45 Avoid overstaffing your stand. It will deter visitors.

IMPROVING YOUR PRESENTATION SKILLS

Effective public relations demands first-rate communication skills, whether one-to-one or one-to-100. Learn to prepare your presentations with care, conquer your nerves, and appraise your performance honestly after the event.

46 Prepare cue cards to remind you of your main points.

47 Avoid a rushed ending by pacing your speech.

48 Deliver your talk in a style that will be appropriate to your audience.

PREPARING TO PRESENT

Few of us are gifted with a natural talent for public speaking. For most people, a successful presentation relies on careful planning and preparation. Start by finding out as much as you can about those you will be addressing, so that you can pitch your talk at the right level. How large will your audience be? Will participants be there by choice? Do they have knowledge of the subject? What is their age and sex? Do they have any relevant affiliations? Think about your style of delivery: should it be light and anecdotal, or serious and academic?

RESEARCHING THE DETAIL

To help you face your audience with confidence, research your venue. Find out how the room will be organized. Will seating be set out theater-style, around a table, or in a horseshoe shape? Having done your research, concentrate on your speech. Define the purpose and intended outcome of your talk, decide on a theme, gather the facts you need, and organize them into a logical structure. Break the talk into manageable chunks. Prepare notes or cue cards and organize handouts or visual aids.

POINTS TO REMEMBER

- If public speaking is a significant part of your job, a training course in presentation skills may be worthwhile.
- Great care should be taken with style and appearance (they account for around 92 percent of the impact you make).
- Visual clues from the audience should be acted upon.

THINGS TO DO

1. Find out if you are being asked to make a speech, give a talk, or lead a discussion.
2. Find out whether the event is formal or informal.
3. Ask how much time you will have.
4. Find out how large the audience will be.

DEVELOPING YOUR OWN STYLE

Truly successful speakers have a strong presence and unique style, and it can be tempting to try to emulate them. However, it is important to develop a style that is natural for you. If you feel comfortable, you will come across as sincere, which will help you win over audiences. Ensure that your style is not patronizing. Use everyday words and phrases. Try to be yourself and imagine that you are talking to just one other person, not a crowd. Speak with immense enthusiasm, even passion. Convey feeling. Remember that enthusiasm is contagious, so spread it to your audience.

Eye contact establishes positive rapport

Relaxed body language conveys confidence

Open jacket presents an image of honesty

Open hand gesture indicates integrity

▲ **APPEARING CONFIDENT**

A confident stance establishes credibility. Speak at a natural pace and aim to maintain eye contact with your audience.

▲ **LOOKING AND FEELING AT EASE**

Relaxed body language conveys honesty and openness. Pause between main points to gauge reactions to your speech.

▲ **USING HAND GESTURES**

Open-handed gestures can help to emphasize key points. Make good use of them to draw the entire audience into the presentation.

31

49 If you are using a microphone, avoid hiding behind it.

50 Remember to smile – but only when it feels natural to do so.

COPING WITH NERVES

It is natural to be nervous at the prospect of facing an audience, no matter how small. In fact, the rush of adrenaline that results from nervousness helps you cope with the stresses of a presentation. However, excessive nerves need to be dealt with. Confidence in your knowledge of the subject can act as a nerve-calmer. Rehearse beforehand to help reassure yourself that you can do it. Practice relaxation breathing techniques so that you are able to control and steady your breathing when the adrenaline kicks in. Use some of your nervous energy to enliven your speech. Take a deep breath before you begin, and have a glass of water at your side to deal with dryness of the mouth. Sometimes it can help to tell your audience that you are feeling a little nervous; this can act as an icebreaker and assist in winning their goodwill.

FACING THE AUDIENCE

The first few minutes of a talk are the most difficult. Survive these, and it can only get easier. Welcome your audience and establish a rapport. Make eye contact to help establish and maintain their interest. Run through the proposed content as part of your introduction. Tell your audience when you will finish, whether there will be any breaks, and whether you will be providing handouts and taking questions. Pace yourself. By the time you complete your introduction, your nerves will have calmed. Immediately after your talk, assess your performance. What did you do well? Where could you improve? Follow up any undertakings made, such as sending out further information.

51 Begin by showing your warmth, friendliness, and enthusiasm.

DOS AND DON'TS

✔ Do dress for the occasion.

✔ Do adopt a positive and confident pose.

✔ Do speak up so that the audience can hear you clearly.

✔ Do finish on time.

✘ Don't use distracting mannerisms.

✘ Don't ramble.

✘ Don't use jargon that is unfamiliar to the audience.

✘ Don't use too many statistics.

USING VISUAL AIDS EFFECTIVELY

VISUAL AID

POINTS TO NOTE

OVERHEAD PROJECTORS
Colorful images for overhead projectors are easily created using inexpensive software. These are useful for showing text, but photographs may not reproduce so well.

- All overheads should have a similar visual style for clarity and cohesion.
- Lower-case lettering is far easier to read than capitals.
- A transparency should be informative, but not crammed with too much detail.

FLIP-CHART
A useful supplementary aid, this is ideal for recording an audience's brainstorming contributions, summarizing action points, and explaining ideas visually.

- Sheets should be prepared in advance, using illustrations to explain key points.
- Important points can be emphasized with color.
- Everyone in the audience must be able to see the flip-chart clearly.

SLIDE PROJECTOR
This is useful when you need to show high quality photographs, since slides are clearer (and more costly) than transparencies.

- Slides should be arranged in order in a slide box prior to your speech.
- Lower lighting levels are needed than for an overhead projector.
- Operating a projector may require some practice prior to your presentation.

LAPTOP COMPUTER
A personal computer with presentation software enables you to prepare visuals and accompanying speaker's notes and handouts in a few easy steps.

- A laptop can be connected to a special projector, enabling slides to be displayed at the click of a mouse.
- High quality graphics may be quickly and inexpensively prepared, and existing slides amended with ease and speed.

VIDEOS
These can be a powerful supplement to a talk. Use videos to show short, live-action images, as well as to spark discussion and debate.

- A video should not take the place of a presentation.
- Videos should be kept short, lasting no longer than about 10 minutes.
- The decision to show a video before or after the presentation may affect its impact.

DEVELOPING AN INTERNET SITE

With literally millions of people logging on to travel in cyberspace, a website is fast becoming an essential communication tool. Establish an informative, persuasive site to help you communicate with your target audiences.

52 Keep an eye on other websites and adapt ideas for your own.

53 Ensure that any graphics used are fast-loading.

54 Make sure that you include your website address in all publicity.

ESTABLISHING A WEBSITE

A professional website can improve your image and enhance communication. If your organization does not already have a website, give some serious thought to creating one. Your public might draw unflattering conclusions from the fact that you are not represented in cyberspace. Although you can buy or download software that will help you create a site, remember that your site will form an important part of your corporate image, so it should look professional. Avoid creating a site that could be seen as amateurish. Unless you have the skills in-house, commission a professional website designer.

BRIEFING A ▶ WEB DESIGNER

Decide how you intend to use your site. Do you want to inform or educate, build awareness or campaign on an issue? The purpose will dictate the content. Brief your designer on the purpose of the site so that it can be tailor-made for your needs.

PR manager points out website features she would like to see incorporated

DEVELOPING AN INTEGRATED WEBSITE

Website content is often seen as the domain of the marketing department, making it consumer- and sales-driven. Ensure that your organization's website is also PR-driven. Create an area for the media with press releases, downloadable pictures, and background information. Many journalists look first to the internet to find out about an organization. Make access easy (and content relevant) for analysts and investors. Help your marketing colleagues see that your website can be used to persuade and influence a wide audience. Ensure that your website design exploits the interactive nature of the internet and enables a two-way flow of messages. Listening to your target audience is as important as talking to them.

DOS AND DON'TS

✔ Do ask your target audience what they want from your site – and keep the information on it up to date.

✔ Do feature changing attractions to tempt visitors back to your site.

✘ Do not allow graphics to dominate at the expense of content – a website is a communications tool.

✘ Do not overload your home page with information; it will deter visitors from exploring your site.

CREATING AN EFFECTIVE WEBSITE

Commission website design

Test the new site for usability

Go "live" and publicize the site

Collect feedback on the site

Amend your site accordingly

Refresh and update the website regularly

WRITING FOR THE INTERNET

Reading on-screen is much harder than reading text on paper. Tests have shown that on-screen reading is, in fact, 25 percent slower. Bear this is mind when writing material for your website. Use short, uncomplicated sentences. One-third to one-half of a page of 8½ x 11 paper can be seen on-screen at a time. Make your site more enticing by breaking up text into manageable chunks and by using plenty of bulletpoints. Surfers dislike scrolling through dense screens of text.

HANDLING CRISES

Crisis management is an essential PR skill. A well-managed crisis can result in an enhanced image rather than a damaged one. Identify potential crises, draw up contingency plans, and you will be able to keep a calm head if disaster strikes.

55 Issue frequent briefings to dispel rumor and speculation.

56 Produce a comprehensive list of potential crises.

BEING PREPARED FOR CRISES

Every organization is a target for crisis. It may come in the shape of fraud; a leak of sensitive information; a hostile takeover bid; robbery; a dangerous product or design fault; sabotage; blackmail; kidnapping; boycotts; natural disaster such as flooding; environmental damage and pollution; or accidents, such as a fatal factory fire. Crises can strike at any time, yet, despite their unpredictable nature, they can be planned for. Examine your vulnerabilities and take preemptive action to reduce risk by strengthening your organization. Identify all the things that could go wrong within your organization, however unlikely.

57 Decide whether you will need legal advisers to guard against litigation.

DRAWING UP A CRISIS PLAN

Plan for every contingency and be ready to respond proactively. Take your list of potential disasters and draw up a crisis plan for each scenario. Include information on what action will be taken by whom to inform relevant staff, official bodies, the media, and the public. Do not limit training to head office staff; if a crisis happens in another location, staff there will have to cope with the initial impact. Plan for every eventuality.

Team member makes note of who to contact in an emergency

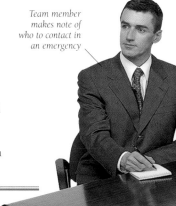

THINGS TO DO

1. Show genuine sympathy to victims, families, and friends if there has been any harm to people.

2. State your concern if there has been harm to property.

3. Promise a full inquiry.

4. Outline the steps that you have taken to rectify the situation.

▼ PLANNING FOR A CRISIS

Bring together members of your crisis team to present roles and responsibilities and discuss necessary action. Such in-depth planning can increase your chances of a positive outcome.

IMPLEMENTING THE ACTION PLAN

However carefully you have planned, when disaster strikes, stress levels will be far higher than experienced during dry runs. It is important to select members of a crisis team for their ability to remain calm and in control while under pressure. This skill may be stretched to the limit. Every member should have a copy of the crisis plan and be aware of what is expected of them, what the boundaries are, and who is in charge. You may need to set up toll-free helplines; organize a product recall, including media advertising and mailshots to product owners; or you may need to hold a press conference on very short notice. Your crisis manual should contain details of how to implement these key crisis actions, making your task more straightforward and enabling you to carry it out with minimum delay.

Manager explains each step of crisis action plan

Team member is allocated role of official spokesperson in the event of crisis

58 Use your website to commmunicate during a crisis.

MANAGING THE MEDIA

Disasters make news. Little-known organizations can suddenly find themselves thrust into the limelight for all the wrong reasons. Effective media handling during a crisis is essential if you want to get your message across and help shape a positive image for your organization, even in adversity. Media attention in a crisis may be unavoidable. Draw up a protocol stating who may and may not comment to the media and make staff aware of this before a crisis occurs. Dealing with aggressive, probing journalists is difficult, so ensure that all spokespeople have undergone media training and know how to field difficult questions. In your crisis manual, list likely tricky questions, as well as good answers to them. Decide how you want to handle the media. You may want to hold a media conference or briefing, or just issue press statements and news releases. Your approach may be proactive, or you may choose to reactively respond to media inquiries. There is no one right way because each crisis demands its own approach.

PR manager reads newspaper allegations that her organization has handled crisis unsympathetically

Manager is pleased with the good press her company has received

59 Learn from other companies that are managing crises.

BENEFITING FROM ▶ CRISIS TRAINING

Having been trained in how to deal with a crisis, Tom, Caitlin, and Peter knew exactly what to do when a serious situation occurred. As a result, the crisis was dealt with swiftly and effectively, with no long-term damage to the company's reputation.

CASE STUDY

Tom, a night security guard at a cookie factory, received a telephone call from a journalist seeking a response to a report that glass had been found in one of the company's cookies. Tom contacted Caitlin, the company press officer, at home. She immediately issued a holding statement, which had been precleared by the company lawyers and chief executive. Next she contacted everyone on her crisis list to inform them, including Peter, the production manager. Peter halted production, notified wholesalers, and organized a product recall. Caitlin placed ads in the national press asking people to return packets labeled batch 201, issued press releases, and posted instructions on the company website. Customers returning packets gave their details and were sent a personalized letter of apology and an impressive goody bag as compensation.

LOOKING AFTER EMPLOYEES

Staff are an important audience in their own right, so make sure that you keep them informed during a crisis. Brief employees during a major crisis so that they are up to date on what happened and why. Hold regular briefings to keep them updated on the situation. Use the company intranet, issue memos, or hold meetings. When the crisis has abated, do not overlook the possible effects of crisis upon staff. Depending on the nature of the incident, they may be upset and traumatised. Assist employees in dealing with what may have been a difficult or anxious situation. If appropriate, offer some time off work, provide stress counseling, or find other ways to assist affected staff.

60 Following a crisis, be sure to debrief staff and review and refine your crisis procedures.

MANAGING CRISES EFFECTIVELY

Identify potential crises and take preemptive action

Draw up crisis action plans for every scenario

Train relevant staff in crisis management skills

Rehearse for crisis situations and test procedures

When crisis strikes, implement your action plan

Review procedures and rebuild any damage to reputation

WORKING WITH THE MEDIA

Media management is a core PR skill. Build strong relationships with journalists, organize successful media events, and monitor coverage to ensure that your message is being conveyed.

MAKING FRIENDS WITH THE MEDIA

Good media contacts often result in better media coverage. Get to know key journalists, and make sure that they know you. Then use your contacts ruthlessly to help you secure excellent coverage for your organization.

61 Understand how people in the press, radio, and television work.

SECURING ATTENTION

Adopting a proactive approach to media management enables you to build and enhance your profile, promote products, present your case, or simply inform the public, politicians, and trade and professional audiences. Reactive media relations leave you responding to other people's stories. Get to know who's who: once media people start looking to you for help with stories, you'll know you have established a good relationship.

62 Familiarize yourself with the news coverage of target publications.

BUILDING RELATIONSHIPS

Organizations with good media contacts and strong, long-term relations with media personnel attract more coverage in general, and more positive coverage in particular. Watch television, listen to the radio, and read newspapers and magazines so that you are familiar with the style of language used and the types of stories covered. Identify programs and publications likely to be good outlets for your news. Get to know the editor of your local or industry publication. Contact journalists who specialize in your field of work. Find out who runs the newsroom at your local radio station and TV newsroom. Recognize that a good relationship is mutually beneficial. Always be helpful to journalists: return their calls, keep their deadlines, and be nice to them to keep them on your side.

▼ MAKING MEDIA CONTACTS

Draw up a list of journalists and correspondents to make contact with and then telephone to introduce yourself. Invite journalists to lunch or out for coffee so that you can get to know them better. It is important to work hard to create and sustain relationships with your target media.

ORGANIZING MEDIA VISITS

Consider organizing a formal media visit to which you can invite reporters you want to get to know. Organize site or factory visits to demonstrate your work in action. Draw up a program that includes lunch with relevant staff. Brief staff on what they can and cannot say over lunch, bearing in mind that many reporters pick up their best stories thanks to loose talk over a bottle of wine. Line up a good story for them to take away, along with a goody bag containing any of your products or a gift. You should not bribe the media, but being mildly generous can help to make them feel better disposed toward you.

POINTS TO REMEMBER

● Journalists are busy people. They need to go away with a good story.

● All journalists like exclusive news, but good stories should be shared, rather than all given to your favorite reporter.

● Journalists may often waste your time, but wasting theirs is never an option if a good relationship is to be maintained.

● Deadlines are vitally important to the media and should be treated with the greatest respect.

ATTRACTING COVERAGE

Favorable media coverage can enhance the reputation of your organization and build credibility with key audiences. Identify newsworthy stories, issue effective news releases, and put together useful media packs to guarantee that you make the headlines.

63 Ask the features editor to consider doing a piece on your organization.

64 Note that letters pages can be an important publicity platform.

65 Use wide margins on releases to give journalists room to make notes.

UNDERSTANDING NEWS RELEASES

The principal way to get on television, radio, or in the press is to issue a news release. A news release is simply your news story, written in a journalistic style. Print and broadcast journalists rely on these releases to help them compile reports, features, and programs. On receiving your release, a news editor will glance at the headline and first paragraph to get the gist of your story. If what he or she sees fails to attract the all-important attention, it will be discarded. It is estimated that this happens to up to 97 percent of releases. To create an attention-grabbing release that will stand out from the hundreds of others received daily, make sure that your story is interesting, unusual, controversial, unique, unexpected, or significant.

HITTING THE HEADLINES

To ensure good media coverage for your organization, issue a news release to publicize anything positive that is likely to attract media attention. This might include:

- new products and services;
- product and service enhancements;
- new staff and promotions;
- the winning of awards and honors;
- new outlets and premises;
- important announcements, such as the creation of new jobs or the opening of a new head office;
- breakthroughs and advancements;
- expansions and takeovers.

NEWS RELEASE

Unless you are placing an embargo on your release, type the words "For immediate use" here

For immediate use   Monday, July 27th

Insert the date of distribution

WORLD'S FIRST ARTIFICIAL SKY

Use a factual but interesting headline

Begin with an interesting story angle

The world's first artificial sky has just been switched on. A British company, LonGlass Limited, has produced a $1.2 million artificial sky for the London offices of New York bank NYCorp.

Computerized lighting behind a glass ceiling creates brightness in the east during the morning, gradually moving west as the day progresses, thus mimicking the real movement of the sun. The whole effect aims to simulate the natural daylight that was lost when a glass atrium at the offices of NYCorp was filled in to create more office space on the floors above.

Use double spacing for the body of your release

Charlie Anderson, Managing Director of LonGlass, says: "This project was not only a major engineering feat, it was a major logistical one too. Because of the bank's need to maintain continuous trading, it was necessary to carry out the work 'after hours' – at night and on weekends."

Include a quotation to make your release look like an authentic media interview

Include any background information in a "Notes to editors" section at the end of your release

NOTES TO EDITORS:

1. LonGlass Limited, which this year celebrates its 50th anniversary, has a turnover of $27 million. Further information about the company is available from its website: www.longlass.co.uk
2. NYCorp was given planning permission to infill the atrium subject to their replacing the lost natural daylight. An artificial sky was the solution.
3. Photographs of the artificial sky, and other projects, can be downloaded from the LonGlass website.

Direct journalists to your website, where they can download relevant photographs and useful background material

Include two contact names with work and home numbers

FOR FURTHER INFORMATION CONTACT:

Jenny Mark, PR Manager, LonGlass Limited, on 020 7177 5433 (office) or 020 8743 4322 (home) or Charlie Anderson, Managing Director, on 020 7177 5434 (office) or 020 7755 4793 (home)

▲ CREATING A SUCCESSFUL RELEASE

A good release may be used as the basis for a report in the media, or it may trigger a call from a reporter wanting to find out more. Ensure your release is cleared for issue by your chief executive or other authorized figure.

66 Cover all the facts and keep your releases succinct.

COVERING THE FIVE "Ws"

Having created a news angle to give your story newsworthiness, make sure your release contains the five "Ws," or key facts around which your story is based. Check that you have covered the following:

● WHO will be doing the activity? It may be an individual, an organization, or both.
● WHAT will they be doing? It may be an activity or an announcement.
● WHEN will they be doing it? State the date and, where appropriate, the time.
● WHERE will the event take place?
● WHY are you doing it? What is the reason?

ISSUING YOUR RELEASE

Once your release has been completed, checked, and authorized by the relevant manager, issue it to your target media. If you are unsure where to send it, look for local media addresses in a telephone directory. For national, trade, technical, and consumer titles, plus radio and TV program details, obtain a specialized media directory. These are expensive, but invaluable if you intend to use media relations as a core plank of your publicity strategy. The directories vary enormously. Some are organized by geographic area, others alphabetically by category (such as aviation, banking, beauty, coin collecting, and so on). Some cover only trade and technical publications, others list only consumer or business titles. Certain directories specialize in the broadcast media, listing programs, names of producers, and brief details on program content.

67 Staple releases to prevent pages from being mislaid in a busy newsroom.

68 Make sure that your release arrives in time to meet deadlines.

POINTS TO REMEMBER

● Releases should be addressed to a named person if they are being sent by mail. Alternatively, they should be marked for the attention of the news editor or other relevant job title.

● If time is short, or a release or media pack is accompanied by an item such as a product sample, it may be advisable to use a courier service.

● Faxes often go astray in large buildings, so this method of issuing releases should be used only if you have a dedicated fax number of the newsroom or relevant journalist.

● IT reporters will prefer to receive releases electronically.

PRODUCING A MEDIA PACK

If you are mounting a campaign or launching a new product, you may need to give journalists a lot more information than can be contained in a single news release. In such cases, you should organize a media pack. Place in the pack a copy of your news release and any other information that will be useful. For example, you might choose to include background information on your organization, campaign, or product. Case histories, biographies of key personnel, factsheets, a list of frequently asked questions (with answers), and photographs can all form part of a press pack. Product samples, too, can be included. Media packs can be sent to journalists or handed out at a media event such as a news conference, press visit, or photo op.

SECURING COVERAGE FROM DIFFERENT MEDIA

MEDIUM	WAYS TO SECURE COVERAGE
TELEVISION This is a fast-moving, visual medium screening only stories that work well on the small screen.	Aim to create interest with children, animals, costumes, props, and colorful backdrops or interesting venues. Select TV spokespeople with care, since some people are more "telegenic" than others.
RADIO As an aural medium, radio relies on the spoken word and on sound effects.	Think how your story will sound, and what you can do to enhance its listenability. Local stations will want local stories, while national ones usually want material with nationwide significance.
PRESS National papers use national stories, or highly unusual local ones. Local papers look for a strong local angle.	Secure national coverage by stressing the scale or significance of your story. For the local press, look out for ways to identify and emphasize the local angle, perhaps by quoting a local manager.
MAGAZINES Stories have a relevant consumer focus or, for specialized titles, one that will appeal to its specific market.	Avoid technical data and concentrate on the significance to the public or the special interest group. Make an early approach, since these publications usually have long lead times.

ORGANIZING A NEWS CONFERENCE

Arrange a conference only when your news is likely to generate considerable media interest – when you are announcing widescale job losses, for example, or announcing significant good news, such as a new factory with an accompanying jobs boost. The idea is to bring everyone together – the media and key representatives from your company – so that you can deal with the announcement and any follow-up interviews at the same time. Have quiet rooms available for media interviews after the event, and ensure that staff giving interviews are fully briefed. Organizing a news conference is time-consuming, and the event itself can be stressful, so ensure that yours will be justified before calling one. If a news release will do the job just as well, send the release – and save time and trouble.

69 Avoid jargon in news releases, unless for the trade press.

70 List your company's experts, and areas of expertise, for your target media.

GIVING MEDIA INTERVIEWS

Being interviewed by the media can be a nerve-wracking business. Prepare well and learn how to respond to difficult questions to ensure that your interview presents you and your organization in a professional and favorable light.

71 Write notes for radio interviews on cue cards – paper will rustle.

72 Avoid distracting mannerisms, such as fiddling with your clothing.

73 Speak in usable, distinct soundbites to help get your message across.

PREPARING FOR A RADIO OR TV INTERVIEW

Broadcast interviews often cause more anxiety than press interviews, but generally there is no need for the extra fear that they tend to generate. Unless an interview is being broadcast live, you do not need to worry too much because it is usually possible to have a question re-asked and re-recorded so that you can offer a more succinct, or a more comprehensive, answer. On most occasions, the interviewer wants to show you at your best, so it is in their interest to relax you and to help you give good answers. Only if you are the villain of the piece will you be given a hard time. To prepare for an interview and build confidence, run through likely questions with a colleague.

◀ **MANAGING A HOSTILE INTERVIEW**
Sometimes your organization will attract media attention when you would rather it did not. It might be that you are laying off staff, closing a factory, or that some crisis has occurred. When faced with cameras, tape recorders, and hostile reporters, keep calm, make sure that you get your key points across, and then bring the interview firmly to a conclusion.

HANDLING DIFFICULT QUESTIONS

Interviewers generally ask questions designed to get interviewees to respond in an interesting, illuminating, lively, animated, or entertaining way. Rigorous or aggressive questioning may be encountered when your organization has done something unacceptable. Decide in advance what you are willing to say and what you will not reveal. Consider how you will handle difficult questions and practice your answers. When posed a tricky question, never say "No comment." This indicates that you have something to hide. Avoid sounding evasive. Concentrate on getting your points across, if necessary by re-interpreting the interviewer's questions. If asked how you feel about laying off employees, focus on the positive, such as the help you are offering staff in securing new jobs. Stress, for example, that all employees will receive paid time off to attend job interviews, as well as free outplacement advice.

▼ RECOGNIZING A GOOD SPOKESPERSON

Most organizations have at least one official spokesperson. Make sure that anyone who will be speaking on your company's behalf has the requisite skills and the appropriate personality to do a good job.

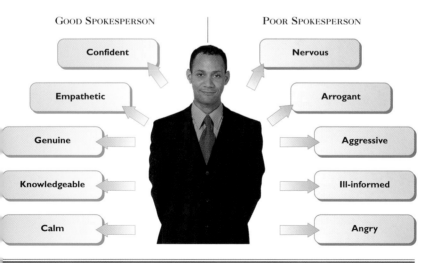

GOOD SPOKESPERSON | POOR SPOKESPERSON

Confident	Nervous
Empathetic	Arrogant
Genuine	Aggressive
Knowledgeable	Ill-informed
Calm	Angry

GETTING PHOTOGRAPHS PUBLISHED

A good photograph is an excellent publicity vehicle. Learn how to create a viable photo opportunity by identifying the elements that comprise a good photo story. Then contact picture editors to "sell" the idea, or commission your own press shots.

74 Whenever your company creates news, consider its picture potential.

WRITING AN EFFECTIVE PHOTO OP NOTICE ▼
To invite photographers to attend a photo op, send them a notice. Shown here is the type of photo op that would merit TV coverage. In this case, radio would be invited too, as the material – music and screaming fans – would make excellent listening for pop stations.

ORGANIZING A PHOTO OP

A photo opportunity (or photo op) is an event that you organize to try to attract press photographers. TV cameras may be invited too, if the event merits it. Produce a photo op notice and send it to the picture desk at your target publications about one week before the event. If a paper regards your photo op as worth considering, it will include it in its picture diary. Bear in mind, however, that this is no guarantee of attendance, particularly if a more newsworthy event occurs in the intervening period.

PHOTO OP   Issued July 10

CHART-TOPPING BAND LIGHTENING TO OPEN RECORD STORE
The chart-topping band Lightening will be in Anytown, performing their hit single *Heartbreak* to shoppers and opening a new record store.

PROGRAM
10 a.m.	Band arrives by stretch limousine, to be greeted by screaming fans
10.30 a.m.	Band performs hit single *Heartbreak* on the sidewalk outside Vinyl Groove
10.35 a.m.	Johnny Splitz, lead singer with Lightening, will officially open the store
10.40 a.m.	The band will sign autographs in the store for the awaiting fans

Date: Tuesday, July 18th Time: 10 a.m. start
Venue: Vinyl Groove Record Store, 27 Main Street, Anytown

YOU ARE INVITED TO SEND A PHOTOGRAPHER
For further information contact: Jenny Stone, store manager, Vinyl Groove 0160 122 5567 (store) or 0160 556 3232 (home) Zak McClone, agent for Lightening 0998 678 4356 (office) or 070 765438 (mobile)

Include a factual headline

Begin with a short paragraph explaining what is happening and why

If appropriate, include a program of events

State where and when the event will be

ISSUING YOUR OWN PHOTOGRAPHS

Local newspapers, trade publications, and some consumer magazines will consider using high quality photographs that are supplied to them. To ensure that your photographs are of an acceptable quality and composition, make sure that you use a professional freelance press photographer who thoroughly understands the needs of the print media. Where appropriate, issue photographs with news releases. Alternatively, state in your news release that photos are available for downloading from your website. Ensure that any photos you issue are clearly captioned on the back. State who or what is shown on the photograph, listing people left to right. Never write directly on the back of the photograph, as this may damage it. Always write your caption on an adhesive label and then attach it.

75 Avoid shots of products on their own, unless for trade publications.

If you have a news release explaining the story, give a copy to the photographer

GETTING THE BEST ► FROM A PHOTO OP

Greet photographers when they arrive at a photo op, explain the purpose of the event, and tell them who or what is available to be photographed.

Introduce the photographer to participants in the photo op

76 Use props or backgrounds to make pictures more interesting.

MONITORING MEDIA COVERAGE

Having succeeded in getting news stories into print or onto film, the next step is to ensure that your organization is being publicized consistently in a positive light. Keep notes of any media contact, track media coverage, and evaluate your work.

> **77** Research software that can help you evaluate media coverage.

LOGGING MEDIA CALLS

KEEPING A MEDIA LOG ▼
Make your logging task easier by drawing up a form to record details of who called and what the outcome was. Complete a log sheet after each call, and make a copy for colleagues who need to know about the call.

The harder you work at raising your company's profile, the more likely it is that you will attract an increased number of calls from the media. Aim to log these calls so that you have a reliable record of reactive media responses. Take a note of who calls, the publication or program they represent, and the nature of their inquiry. Also record your response or any statement issued. Ask when the piece is being run and when it appears, check that you have been represented fairly.

Write down what the journalist wants to know and why

MEDIA LOG

Name of journalist	Publication/program
Contact phone number	Contact fax number
Date of call	Time of call
Call taken by	Response needed by
Nature of inquiry	
Response	
Response issued by	Method

Ask when a response is needed to avoid missing media deadlines

Make a note of what you said in response to the call – if you issued a written response, attach it to the log

Insert name of person providing the response

State whether the call was dealt with there and then, or handled in a follow-up phone call, by mail, email, or fax

TRACKING COVERAGE

Every time you issue a news release or photo op notice, keep a copy for your files. Attach to it a distribution list and compare actual media coverage against this list to work out your "hit" rate. If most of your releases are being used, you are probably being highly effective. If only a small percentage of releases are being published or aired, investigate why. Are you missing deadlines, issuing weak releases, or targeting the wrong media? Call some names on your distribution list and see if you can find out.

78 Consider using a press clippings bureau to help you monitor the coverage you receive.

79 Record TV news to see if messages are well conveyed.

80 Keep a scrap book of press clippings for your archive.

USING A BUREAU

Consider outsourcing media monitoring to a specialized bureau. These companies will issue press clippings, audio tapes of radio coverage, video tapes of television coverage, and transcripts of broadcast coverage. Many also offer an evaluation service. You may need one bureau for press and another for broadcast monitoring, as not all bureaus handle both. Press clippings bureaus often charge a monthly retainer or reading fee, and an amount per cutting. Broadcast monitoring firms do not usually charge a retainer.

EVALUATING COVERAGE

Organizations once used quantitative rather than qualitative measures for assessing their media effectiveness. A thick bundle of press cuttings represented success. Today, this measure is seen as one-dimensional since it fails to distinguish between positive and negative coverage. Your evaluation should assess each piece of media coverage to ascertain whether the messages conveyed are positive, negative, or neutral. Also take into account the value of successfully keeping potentially damaging stories out of the media. Effective evaluation relies on the analysis of a combination of factors, namely: frequency (how often the story is repeated); circulation (how many people were reached); and readership (whether the readership is a key audience for your organization).

PRODUCING PUBLICITY

Effective printed materials are key to successful PR. Learn to write powerful copy, commission strong design and photography, and organize quality printing to ensure persuasive results.

THINKING ABOUT PUBLICITY

Producing a PR document, such as a promotional brochure, from scratch can be daunting. To produce publicity material that will attain maximum impact with the minimum of stress, plan throroughly and allow plenty of time.

81 Avoid rushing key decisions – focus on getting them absolutely right.

82 Remember to allow time to evaluate any quotes submitted.

IMPROVING RESULTS

The key to producing effective publicity materials is to adopt an organized approach. Make sure that you allow sufficient time by creating a production schedule setting out deadlines for copy, proofs, and final artwork. Circulate a copy to appropriate colleagues, making it clear who is responsible for each task. Build in a margin of time for delays, and seek competitive quotes from suppliers such as copywriters, photographers, and printers.

▼ PLANNING PUBLICITY

It is easier for the team to produce effective publicity if everyone has a clear vision of what they are aiming for. Work with the team to form a concept for your material, and then explain your ideas to copywriters, designers, and illustrators.

PR executive explains his concept to team members

UNDERSTANDING AIDCA

Every item of publicity you produce should attract attention. Make your publicity attention-grabbing using color, layout, illustration, and text to create an unmissable piece of publicity. Next, maintain interest by holding the attention of the reader with captivating, persuasive, clear, and readable copy. Ease the reading process with thoughtful design and navigational layout. Then create desire. Decide what reader-response you want, and produce publicity designed to elicit that reaction. Having appealed to the heart, now use hard and persuasive facts to build conviction. The final test of successful publicity material is its ability to prompt action. These five stages are known by the acronym AIDCA, standing for attention, interest, desire, conviction, and action.

USING YOUR PUBLICITY

It is not uncommon for organizations to spend considerable sums of money producing quality publicity material, only to leave much of it stacked, unused, in a storeroom. Ensure that your brochures and other materials are distributed to your target audiences. Draw up a distribution plan, and be ready to activate it as soon as your material is ready. Check that staff are aware of new materials and have sufficient supplies to hand out. Take your publicity materials to talks, seminars, and exhibitions. Leave supplies where they will be picked up by your target audience. Aim to make your materials work hard for you.

QUESTIONS TO ASK YOURSELF

Q What publicity material do we need?

Q Why do we need it: is there anything else we can use?

Q How will we use it: will we send material out in mailshots, or simply hand it out?

Q What is purpose of the material: is it meant to publicize or persuade?

Q Who is publicity aimed at, and is there a target delivery date?

WRITING COPY

A few well-chosen words can stir the emotions and even persuade people to adopt a different viewpoint. The art lies in choosing the right words. Effective copy remembers the reader, uses straightforward language, and employs meticulous planning.

83 Write with a real person, rather than an abstract category, in mind.

UNDERSTANDING COPY

Publicity material should be written in a totally new and different language. It is neither business writing nor traditional composition but a style that is creative and rule-breaking. Certain grammatical strictures can be abandoned in the language of copy. As long as communication is not being impeded, it is acceptable to adopt a more relaxed style of writing, something more akin perhaps to the spoken word.

84 Practice writing copy until you feel more comfortable with the style.

DIFFERENTIATING WRITING STYLES

BUSINESS WRITING	COPYWRITING
Uses a formal style and is traditional in its language.	Is informal in style, using contractions such as "you're" and "we'll."
Often uses the "third person," for example "the organization" and "the customer."	Usually makes use of the first and second person, for example, "we" and "you."
Often uses business or company jargon.	Uses plain English at all times.
Often comprises long tracts of text.	Comprises short, readable chunks of text.
Follows strict grammatical rules.	Breaks grammatical rules in a controlled way.
Uses the passive voice.	Uses the active voice.

GETTING STARTED ON YOUR COPY

Jot down your thoughts and ideas

Organize your ideas into clear themes

Arrange your themes in a logical order

Decide on what goes where and the space it should occupy

Sit down and write a first draft

Revise your draft and polish your finished work

85 Identify your audience before setting pen to paper.

CULTURAL DIFFERENCES

Although English is a global language, usage and style differ from one country to another. If expressing dates in numerals, for example, 2.6.01 would be interpreted as June 2, 2001, in the United Kingdom but as February 6, 2001, in the United States. Similarly the French and Germans use a period to group digits in numbers and a comma as the decimal separator, whereas the Anglo-Saxon countries do the opposite, that is 1,000 could mean one (to three decimal places), or one thousand. In Germany and Scandinavia, writers often emphasize points by indenting them on a separate line rather than underlining or italicizing them, which is how important points are often emphasized in the U.S. and the U.K.

USING PLAIN ENGLISH

Organizational jargon is an extremely useful shorthand when confined to communication in-house or with fellow professionals who, as it were, speak the language. However, publicity materials are generally produced for an external audience and should avoid jargon. Jargon-free writing is known as "plain English." It features short, everyday words and brief sentences; unnecessary technical terms and "officialese" are avoided. Plain English follows a clear and logical order that takes into account the needs and interests of the reader. It is a straightforward and transparent style, not a pompous, self-important, and opaque way of writing. Replace cumbersome and clichéd phrases with succinct words: "now" rather than "at this point in time," for example.

86 Use headlines and subheads to break up your body copy.

87 Avoid using dense screens of text, as this will deter readers.

APPLYING COPYWRITING TECHNIQUES

Professional copywriters use a number of techniques to add interest and life to their prose. Rhyme is a much-used technique, as is alliteration (where two or more neighboring words begin with the same sound). Puns (witty plays on words), too, are a popular technique. Good copy has rhythm. A mix of short and longer sentences can help your copy flow. An occasional one-word sentence will provide interest and unexpectedly alter the rhythm in a way that holds a reader's interest. Avoid monotony by inverting sentences and creating a new word order. For example, rather than writing "This year's catalog features a wider range of products than ever and is unmissable," try "With a wider than ever range of products, this year's catalog is unmissable."

FINDING INSPIRATION

When you are under pressure to produce a piece of publicity, it can be difficult to come up with a good idea. The harder you try, the more elusive the idea becomes. Look out for other people's good ideas and build up a collection of inspirational publicity material. When inspiration is lacking, look through your collection to see if it can spark a few ideas. Analyze effective copy and try to identify the techniques the writer has used. See if those techniques can be re-interpreted and re-deployed in your own work. Sometimes inspiration can be found in unexpected places: children's books, giftwrap, greeting cards, and magazines have all served to stimulate creativity. If inspiration still eludes you, try a brainstorming session with colleagues. This may free your mind and help release a good idea.

▼ COLLECTING IDEAS
Build up a scrapbook of inspirational publicity that you can refer to when you need to think up new ideas. Bear in mind that inspiration can sometimes come from unexpected places, such as children's books or greeting cards.

56

REVISING YOUR WORK

Produce a first draft of your publicity material, then put it aside for a day or two. Return to it fresh and your chances of spotting its shortcomings will be increased. Identify areas for improvement, then redraft as necessary. Repeat this process until you are happy with the result. When revising your work, look out for: clichés, repetition of words or phrases, jargon, and redundancy (unnecessary words). Check for lack of consistency. Avoid verbosity, ambiguity, and pomposity. Aim for clarity and brevity. Having reached a version that you feel content with, test your text on a small number of people representative of your target audience. Ask for feedback and amend your copy as necessary.

▼ **MAKING CORRECTIONS**
Each time you make revisions, read through your copy carefully, checking for consistency and clarity as well as for any mistakes in spelling or punctuation. The more professional your publicity is, the more seriously it will be taken.

PR executive cuts extraneous words to tighten up her copy

USING A COPYWRITER

Regard copy as one of the most vital elements of successful publicity materials. Unless you have the utmost confidence in your ability to write good copy, commission a professional copywriter to do the job for you. Copywriters know how to attract and maintain readers' attention and are skilled in translating complex ideas into lively, readable text.

DEALING WITH WRITER'S BLOCK

All writers experience writer's block occasionally, but it is an affliction that strikes inexperienced writers particularly frequently. The main symptom is an inexplicable inability to concentrate or to write. If you do suffer from writer's block, try one of the many techniques guaranteed to help you get started – or finished. Take a break, get some fresh air, or try a change of scene. Find a quiet place to work, or take your writing home with you. Boost your energy levels by running around the block or eating a snack. You will probably be more alert earlier in the working day, so time your copywriting for the morning if writer's block remains a problem.

DESIGNING PUBLICITY

*A*ttractive publicity design is as important as well-written copy. Tackle design in-house, or use a professional graphic designer or illustrator. Know how to brief a designer, check proofs, and assess the effectiveness of the design.

88 Choose a point size large enough for people to able to read easily.

89 Check that the eye can easily follow the design.

DESIGNING IN-HOUSE

With desktop publishing software, basic design is within the realms of any organization. Materials such as invoices, in-house manuals, order forms, and price lists may be easily designed to a professional standard in-house. Keep it simple. Limit yourself to one or two fonts (type faces) and point sizes (type sizes). Use established templates as your basis, but personalize them to fit your corporate style. Attend a desktop publishing (DTP) course if necessary. Technical competence should be accompanied by a good eye for design.

KEEPING YOUR LAYOUTS SIMPLE ▼
Desktop publishing enables users to create professional publicity materials that reinforce corporate identity. Avoid using too many effects and opt for clear, simple layouts.

POOR EXAMPLE

Layout is chaotic and difficult to follow

Too many fonts and point sizes look confusing and messy

Overuse of clipart and heavy borders gives amateurish feel to design

Dark paper detracts from message

GOOD EXAMPLE

Layout and text are clear, readable, and easy to follow

Using fewer fonts and point sizes helps keep the message clear and easily accessible

USING "OVERPRINT" STATIONERY

Overprint stationery enables you to have attractive and professional design without the expense of commissioning original design. Specialized suppliers produce attractive designs of letterheads and business stationery, menus, invoices, leaflets, posters, and other publicity material. This is then overprinted on a laser printer or photocopier with your own text, address, and other information. Slightly more costly are personalized "empty belly" leaflets or posters. Similar in principle to overprint stationery, these are designed just for you and may incorporate your logo and corporate colors.

90 Check that your logo appears on everything you design.

91 Use personalized stationery for professional and quick results.

FINDING A DESIGNER

It is important to use designers wherever possible, since poor design will reflect badly on your reputation. Professional training and know-how enables them to do a better job than even the most avid amateur. If you do not already have a good relationship with a designer, find one you can work with. Use either a design consultant or a freelance. Some designers charge significantly more than others, but quality and price do not always go hand in hand, so shop around. Ask about fees during any initial discussions. Most designers will show you their best work, usually to be found in high-budget, lavish productions. Ask to see examples of both low- and mid-budget work too. Their ability to tackle a low-budget commission well is a good indicator of their general ability and creativity.

MEETING DESIGNERS ▼

Arrange to see three or four designers and look through their portfolios. Select a designer you feel you can work with. Choose one whose work you like, whose style is varied, and who seems to have a good feel for what you are seeking.

Designer explains his areas of expertise

PROVIDING A COMPREHENSIVE DESIGN BRIEF

KEY AREA	WHAT TO COVER IN YOUR BRIEF
AUDIENCE	Explain who the publicity is aimed at. Try to paint a picture of the type of person who will read it.
STYLE	What style are you looking for? Nostalgic? Contemporary? High-tech? Lavish? Explain your ideas fully.
EXTENT	Inform your designer of the number of pages and what size they should be (for example, whether they are 8½ x 11 or 11 x 17).
ILLUSTRATIONS	State whether charts, tables, and other illustrations are required, and tell your designer of photography requirements.
COLORS	State how many colors should be used, and whether there are certain colors to include (such as corporate colors) or avoid.
PAPER	Explain your requirements for a particular type or color of paper, asking your designer for advice and samples if necessary.
SPECIAL EFFECTS	Discuss any special effects required, such as die cutting, spot varnishes, or foil blocking, and ask for your designer's input.

92 Choose artwork that is appropriate for your audience.

93 Use the local art college as a source of design talent.

COMMISSIONING ILLUSTRATION

Graphic designers take text and produce layouts using special computer design packages. Illustrators provide designers with drawings, paintings, and other illustrations, usually produced on paper. Your designer should be able to put you in touch with an illustrator who can produce the style of artwork you are looking for. Like artists, illustrators have their own distinct style – perhaps very detailed and lifelike, or bold abstract work. Ask to see an illustrator's portfolio to satisfy yourself that you like their style.

94 Spot misspellings by reading from right to left.

95 Look through brochures and collect design ideas that appeal.

ESTABLISHING A HOUSE STYLE

To ensure that all your material is seen to come from the same source, establish your own house style. Specify the font and colors to be used. These will probably be taken from your corporate identity. State how large your logo must be (or how small it can go) and where it should be positioned. House style can cover words as well as design. Produce guidelines to ensure consistency. Explain, for example, what the acceptable writing style is, or how words with alternative spellings should be spelled. Give copies to anyone responsible for writing or designing material.

CHECKING PROOFS THOROUGHLY

When checking proofs, there is plenty to watch out for. Often you will find that a word has been repeated. Spelling mistakes may occur. A word may be missed altogether. That is why it is important to read what is there, not what you think is there. Avoid speed reading. Pore over every word. Look for awkward breaks in words. Words may have two spellings: take "high-tech" and "hi-tech." You may use British "ise" endings, as in "utilise," or American "ize," as in "utilize." The golden rule is to be consistent.

▶ ACHIEVING CONSISTENCY
Read all proofs to ensure consistency and accuracy throughout. Correct any spelling variations or inaccurate punctuation, and make sure that any photos and captions have been correctly paired.

Trade show attracts record crowds

This year's popular three-day Forrestville Garden Furniture trade show attracted record crowds of 45,000 at the city's Central Arena. One hundred of California's leading garden furniture manufacturers took part and exhibited their latest designs at the successful show which was organized by Forrest Inc. and promoted by Public Relations consultants Promo. John Smith, Chief Executive of Forrest Inc. said: "It is only the third year we have organized this event and we are all delighted by the record attendance figures. Plans are already in the pipeline for next year's show when we hope to introduce new facilities for our exhibitors and visitors with more onsite catering outlets." Highlights of this year's designs included a glass and plastic multi-colored five-piece table and chair set with inbuilt glass holders as well as a more traditional alpine chalet-styled shed, complete with verandah and fencing – the perfect play house.

Over 40,000 people visited Forrestville Garden Furniture show.

COMMISSIONING PHOTOGRAPHY

Whether you are using pictures on your website or on your publicity materials, products, premises, and people will look their best when photographed by a professional. Build up a stock of good quality photographs that reflect your work.

96 Bear in mind that good photographs can speak louder than words.

97 Ask to see evidence of a photographer's area of expertise.

FINDING A PHOTOGRAPHER

Photographers excel in different areas, so you may have to use different people for different assignments. Some are excellent press photographers, others excel at studio work, and others have a talent for photographing people. Ask about a photographer's area of expertise, look at their portfolios, and judge for yourself.

BRIEFING YOUR PHOTOGRAPHER

Give your photographer a full brief. Begin with the assignment. State locations (and whether indoor or outdoor) and, where necessary, draw up a schedule. List who or what is to be photographed and what you hope to show or to achieve with each shot, then state when you want the job completed. Provide some background material on your company to help the photographer understand your work. Always confirm details in writing, and ask the photographer to assign copyright for pictures to you, also in writing.

▼ **DISCUSSING FORMAT**
Specify the format that you want your photographer to use, for example color transparencies. If you are unsure, explain how you want to use the photos and ask what would be the best format.

USING YOUR OWN PHOTOGRAPHS

Look for opportunities to use your photographs. Incorporate them into exhibition and display boards. Include relevant shots in press packs, use them to illustrate your website, and provide downloadable pictures for media use. Make good use of photographs in publicity materials and incorporate slides into talks and presentations to bring them to life.

98 Ask photographers to confirm shoot details in writing.

USING PICTURE LIBRARIES

You can obtain professional photographs from picture libraries, which provide a choice of literally millions of high-quality images. This is a useful option if you are looking for top quality photos that would be uneconomical to commission yourself, perhaps because an exotic location is required, or models, or special props. Simply describe in as much detail as possible the type of image you want and leave the library to source a selection. Often a small search fee is charged, which is waived if you "buy" the image. Generally, you pay for permission to use an image once, with the fee depending on factors such as where it will appear and how large it will be. Buying sole rights to use a photo is expensive and probably unnecessary. Most picture libraries produce CD-ROM catalogs that give an indication of the pictures they stock. Bear in mind that these contain only a sample of what is on offer, since a CD has room for only a limited number of images.

COMPARING PRICES

Although price should not dictate which photographer you use, it may influence selection to some degree. When asking photographers about their charges, check the following:
- Rate – this may be charged hourly, daily or half-daily, or per assignment;
- Materials – you may be charged extra for film, developing, and contact sheets;
- Expenses – ask what expenses are charged and at what rate, such as mileage and meals;
- Prints – ask the price of different sized prints.

Work out the approximate overall cost of different photographers. A low hourly rate may not ultimately produce a smaller bill.

POINTS TO REMEMBER

- Premises should always be cleaned before a photo shoot.
- Photographs should be as interesting, creative, and imaginative as possible.
- Shots of large crowds or people in meetings should be avoided.
- Photographs should not contain too many different elements.
- A photographic budget can be stretched by anticipating need and taking shots that could be used in the future.

GETTING PUBLICITY PRINTED

*E*very PR executive needs a good working knowledge of print production. Ensure that you know how to select the right printer for the right job, and learn which factors influence cost and how to make savings by undertaking your own print-buying.

99 Check proofs carefully before signing them off for printing.

OBTAINING COMPETITIVE QUOTATIONS

Prepare a short-list of printers

⬇

Draw up a specification detailing your needs

⬇

Ask for a written quote and samples

⬇

Select a printer based on price and quality

⬇

Confirm the job in writing, and state the delivery date and delivery address

CHOOSING A PRINTER

Whenever you use a supplier, make sure that you shop around – not only for the best price, but also for the most appropriate provider for your needs. Most large printing firms employ sales representatives who will be happy to visit you. Find out what equipment and machinery the print firm uses and what it is capable of. Ensure that the representative brings samples. Check that the quality is good. Are colors true? Are documents folded neatly? Are pages stapled, or wire stitched, with precision? Are pages cut square? Usually a rep can arrange for you to visit and to see the printshop in action. This is a good opportunity to introduce yourself to the processes and the jargon, and to ask questions.

DOS AND DON'TS

✔ Do get three quotes for every print job, and tell printers you are doing this.

✔ Do ask for a fully inclusive and itemized quote that also covers any extras.

✘ Do not give work to a printer if you are unhappy with the quality of their samples.

✘ Do not use a printer who took too long to prepare a quote – this signals unreliability.

BUDGETING FOR PRINT

Many factors affect print prices. Internal factors – such as how busy the printer is, or how much they want your business – will have an influence. Then there is the specification or "spec." Certain processes will add to the cost. Full-color printing costs more than two-color printing. The number of pages (extent), the number of copies (run), and the type of paper used (stock) will also affect cost. Special effects and finishes, such as metallic inks, die-cutting, varnishing, laminating, and embossing will inflate the bill. There will be a charge for scanning (converting photographs into a form that enables them to be printed) and for the provision of cromalins (special photographic proofs).

100 Negotiate print quotes downward to ensure that you get the best deal.

USING DIGITAL PRINTING

Traditional printing performed on a printing press is ideal for runs of at least 500: the larger the run, the lower the unit cost. However, for short runs – especially short full-color runs – digital printing is more cost effective. With a press, where the main cost is in setting up the machine, making small runs is uneconomical. Digital printing has no setup costs, so the unit cost for one copy is little different to the unit cost for 1,000. Many printshops offer both forms of printing. Ask which is best for your needs.

UNDERTAKING YOUR OWN PRINT-BUYING

If you do not have time to arrange your own printing, or if print-buying is a new area and you would prefer to gain some experience first, you can ask a graphic designer to organize it for you. In the long term, however, it is cheaper to do your own print-buying. It is standard practice for designers to mark up the cost of printing, usually by about 15 or 20 percent, as a kind of handling fee.

101 Make significant savings by doing your own print-buying.

ASSESSING YOUR PR ABILITY

A thorough understanding of PR techniques will help you to build a good image and protect the reputation of your organization. Test your skills by answering the following questions. If your answer is "Never," mark option 1; if it is "Always," mark option 4, and so on. Add your scores together, and refer to the analysis to see how you fared. Use the answers to identify areas that need improving.

OPTIONS
1 Never
2 Occasionally
3 Frequently
4 Always

1 I always consider the PR implications of actions.

| 1 | 2 | 3 | 4 |

2 I explain to non-PR colleagues the PR implications of their plans.

| 1 | 2 | 3 | 4 |

3 I try to find ways to support marketing activity within my organization.

| 1 | 2 | 3 | 4 |

4 I look for ways to improve communication within my organization.

| 1 | 2 | 3 | 4 |

5 I try to find ways to improve external communication.

| 1 | 2 | 3 | 4 |

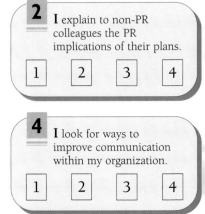

6 I always set objectives for PR activity.

| 1 | 2 | 3 | 4 |

7 I select communications channels with care.

1   2   3   4

8 I define clear messages for each PR initiative.

1   2   3   4

9 I seek to measure the effectiveness of PR activities.

1   2   3   4

10 I ensure that staff information is presented clearly and honestly.

1   2   3   4

11 I consider the impact of all our activities on our reputation.

1   2   3   4

12 I pay attention to the smallest detail when organizing events.

1   2   3   4

13 I select event venues with great care.

1   2   3   4

14 I provide written briefs for event participants.

1   2   3   4

15 I consider the legal and safety issues of any event.

1   2   3   4

16 I set aside time to plan and prepare for talks and presentations.

1   2   3   4

17 I evaluate my performance after giving a presentation.

1 2 3 4

18 I look for opportunities to attract positive media coverage.

1 2 3 4

19 I work hard to build and maintain good relationships with the media.

1 2 3 4

20 I check press releases to ensure that the five "Ws" are covered.

1 2 3 4

21 I prepare thoroughly for media interviews.

1 2 3 4

22 I try to anticipate tricky media questions.

1 2 3 4

23 I examine events for their photo opportunity potential.

1 2 3 4

24 I log all media calls.

1 2 3 4

25 I calculate the hit rate of news releases.

1 2 3 4

26 I evaluate media coverage.

1 2 3 4

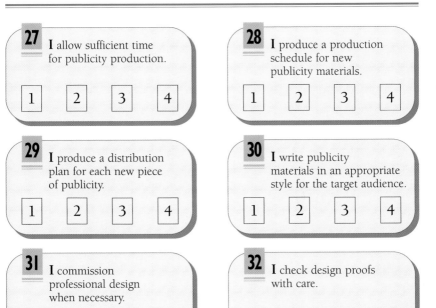

27 I allow sufficient time for publicity production.

1 2 3 4

28 I produce a production schedule for new publicity materials.

1 2 3 4

29 I produce a distribution plan for each new piece of publicity.

1 2 3 4

30 I write publicity materials in an appropriate style for the target audience.

1 2 3 4

31 I commission professional design when necessary.

1 2 3 4

32 I check design proofs with care.

1 2 3 4

ANALYSIS

Now that you have completed the self-assessment, add up your total score and check your performance. Whatever level of success you have achieved, there is always room for improvement. Identify your weakest areas, then refer to the relevant sections of this book, where you will find practical advice and tips to help you establish and hone your PR skills.

32–63: You need to take a more organized, systematic, sustained, and proactive approach to improve the effectiveness of your PR activity.

64–95: Some of your PR activity is having a positive impact on your organization's reputation, but you need to develop your skills to become more strategic in approach.

96–128: You are thorough, professional, strategic, and are achieving considerable success. Keep it up.

INDEX

ACKNOWLEDGMENTS

AUTHOR'S ACKNOWLEDGMENTS

I would like to thank everyone who helped on this book, including Ray Gaulke and John Elsasser of the Public Relations Society of America, Cathy Melnicki at DK Inc., and Susan Shayshutt of the Institute of Public Relations.

PUBLISHER'S ACKNOWLEDGMENTS

Dorling Kindersley would like to thank the following for their help and participation in producing this book:

Photographer Steve Gorton.

Models Tracey Allanson, Roger Andre, Angela Cameron, Brent Clark, Lorraine Evans, Emma Harris, Roger Mundy, Kaz Takabatake, Suki Tan, Peter Taylor, Anastasia Vengeroua, Dominica Warburton, Ann Winterborn.

Make-up Janice Tee.

Picture research Cheryl Dubyk-Yates.
Picture library assistance Melanie Simmonds.

Editorial Alison Bolus, Fiona Wild.
Indexer Hilary Bird.

AUTHOR'S BIOGRAPHY

Moi Ali runs her own public relations and marketing company, specializing in clients with limited budgets – in particular small businesses and charities. She is a regular contributor to marketing and PR journals and is the author of a number of books, including *Practical Marketing and PR for the Small Business*, and *The DIY Guide to Marketing for Charities*.